Project Management
NOTEBOOK

Owner

Date/s

Details

Published by **STANFORD DOUGLAS**

Copyright © 2021 Stanford Douglas

With thanks to **Martin Johnson**
for his project management experience.

ISBN 9798487254719 (Paperback)

INDEX

Continued on page 4

NOTES

-
-
-
-
-
-
-
-
-
-
-
-
-
-
-
-
-
-
-
-
-
-

DEFINE PROJECT SCOPE AND GOALS

AGREED PROJECT GOALS

RESOURCES

Name   Email   Phone

Responsibilities

Name   Email   Phone

Responsibilities

Name   Email   Phone

Responsibilities

Name   Email   Phone

Responsibilities

Name   Email   Phone

Responsibilities

Name   Email   Phone

Responsibilities

Name   Email   Phone

Responsibilities

Name   Email   Phone

Responsibilities

TIMELINE

TIMELINE

TIMELINE

TIMELINE

TIMELINE NOTES

DEPENDENCIES

DEPENDENCIES

BUDGET

No	Item	Estimated	Actual	TOTAL
	(Sub total carried forward)/**TOTAL**			

No	Item	Estimated	Actual	TOTAL
	Sub total cf/TOTAL			

BUDGET

No	Item	Estimated	Actual	TOTAL
	(Sub total carried forward)/**TOTAL**			

No	Item	Estimated	Actual	TOTAL
	TOTAL			

STAKEHOLDER ANALYSIS

Who

What

Who

What

Who

What

Who

What

Who

What

Who

What

Who

What

Who

What

STAKEHOLDER ANALYSIS

Who

What

Who

What

Who

What

Who

What

Who

What

Who

What

Who

What

Who

What

MATRIX

NOTES

NOTES

_____

_____

_____

_____

MIND MAP 1

MIND MAP 2

RISKS

Risk
_____

Mitigating action/s
_____
_____
_____

Risk
_____

Mitigating action/s
_____
_____
_____

Risk
_____

Mitigating action/s
_____
_____
_____

Risk
_____

Mitigating action/s
_____
_____
_____

Risk

Mitigating action/s

Risk

Mitigating action/s

Risk

Mitigating action/s

Risk

Mitigating action/s

RISKS

Risk

Mitigating action/s

Risk

Mitigating action/s

Risk

Mitigating action/s

Risk

Mitigating action/s

Risk

Mitigating action/s

Risk

Mitigating action/s

Risk

Mitigating action/s

Risk

Mitigating action/s

ACTIONS

No	Action	Responsible/owner	When due

No	Action	Responsible/owner	When due

ACTIONS

No	Action	Responsible/owner	When due

No	Action	Responsible/owner	When due

ACTIONS

No	Action	Responsible/owner	When due

No	Action	Responsible/owner	When due

MEETING SCHEDULES

Meeting title	
Date of first meeting	
Chair	
Co-chair	
Purpose of meeting	
Frequency	
Preferred type	◯ Face to face　　◯ Telephone　　◯ Online. . . . .
Attendees	

Meeting title	
Date of first meeting	
Chair	
Co-chair	
Purpose of meeting	
Frequency	
Preferred type	◯ Face to face　　◯ Telephone　　◯ Online. . . . .
Attendees	

Meeting title	
Date of first meeting	
Chair	
Co-chair	
Purpose of meeting	
Frequency	
Preferred type	◯ Face to face ◯ Telephone ◯ Online. . . . .
Attendees	

Meeting title	
Date of first meeting	
Chair	
Co-chair	
Purpose of meeting	
Frequency	
Preferred type	◯ Face to face ◯ Telephone ◯ Online. . . . .
Attendees	

MEETING SCHEDULES

Meeting title	
Date of first meeting	
Chair	
Co-chair	
Purpose of meeting	
Frequency	
Preferred type	◯ Face to face ◯ Telephone ◯ Online. . . . .
Attendees	

Meeting title	
Date of first meeting	
Chair	
Co-chair	
Purpose of meeting	
Frequency	
Preferred type	◯ Face to face ◯ Telephone ◯ Online. . . . .
Attendees	

Meeting title	
Date of first meeting	
Chair	
Co-chair	
Purpose of meeting	
Frequency	
Preferred type	◯ Face to face ◯ Telephone ◯ Online. . . . .
Attendees	

Meeting title	
Date of first meeting	
Chair	
Co-chair	
Purpose of meeting	
Frequency	
Preferred type	◯ Face to face ◯ Telephone ◯ Online. . . . .
Attendees	

MEETING SCHEDULES

Meeting title	
Date of first meeting	
Chair	
Co-chair	
Purpose of meeting	
Frequency	
Preferred type	○ Face to face ○ Telephone ○ Online. . . . .
Attendees	

Meeting title	
Date of first meeting	
Chair	
Co-chair	
Purpose of meeting	
Frequency	
Preferred type	○ Face to face ○ Telephone ○ Online. . . . .
Attendees	

Meeting title	
Date of first meeting	
Chair	
Co-chair	
Purpose of meeting	
Frequency	
Preferred type	◯ Face to face ◯ Telephone ◯ Online. . . . .
Attendees	

Meeting title	
Date of first meeting	
Chair	
Co-chair	
Purpose of meeting	
Frequency	
Preferred type	◯ Face to face ◯ Telephone ◯ Online. . . . .
Attendees	

MEETING SCHEDULES

Meeting title	
Date of first meeting	
Chair	
Co-chair	
Purpose of meeting	
Frequency	
Preferred type	◯ Face to face ◯ Telephone ◯ Online.............................
Attendees	

Meeting title	
Date of first meeting	
Chair	
Co-chair	
Purpose of meeting	
Frequency	
Preferred type	◯ Face to face ◯ Telephone ◯ Online.............................
Attendees	

Meeting title	
Date of first meeting	
Chair	
Co-chair	
Purpose of meeting	
Frequency	
Preferred type	◯ Face to face ◯ Telephone ◯ Online. . . . .
Attendees	

Meeting title	
Date of first meeting	
Chair	
Co-chair	
Purpose of meeting	
Frequency	
Preferred type	◯ Face to face ◯ Telephone ◯ Online. . . . .
Attendees	

MEETING PLANNER

Date/s:			

MEETING PLANNER

Date/s:				

MEETING NOTES

MEETING NOTES

MEETING NOTES

MEETING NOTES

MEETING NOTES

MEETING NOTES

MEETING NOTES

MEETING NOTES

MEETING NOTES

MEETING NOTES

MEETING NOTES

MEETING NOTES

MEETING NOTES

MEETING NOTES

Made in United States
Troutdale, OR
04/27/2024

19491995R00080